DAILY Reading Plan & Journal

Read the Bible Cover to Cover THIS YEAR

2019 AMPC Bible
Daily Reading Plan & Journal
Read The Bible Cover to Cover This Year

Original first edition
Copyright January 21, 2019
by ReadioActive Publishing, LLC
Printed in the United States of America

ISBN-10: 1-68455-006-8
ISBN-13: 978-1-68455-006-7

All rights reserved. No part of this publication may be reproduced, transmitted, downloaded, decompiled, reverse engineered, or stored in or introduced into any information storage and retrieval system, in any form or by any means, whether electronic or mechanical, without the written permission of the publisher. The scanning, uploading, and distribution of this book via the internet or any other means without the permission of the publisher is illegal and punishable by law.

Reviewers may quote brief excerpts in printed reviews.

Scripture references are from the King James Version of the Bible rights in the United States are Public Domain.

Scripture references from The Authorized (King James) Version. Rights in the Authorized Version in the United Kingdom are vested in the Crown. Reproduced by permission of the Crown's patentee, Cambridge University Press

Scripture quotations marked (AMPCE) are taken from the Amplified Bible, Copyright © 1954, 1958, 1962, 1964, 1965, 1987 by The Lockman Foundation. Used by permission.

Company and product names mentioned herein are the trademarks or registered trademarks of their respective owners.

Published by ReadioActive Publishing, LLC
https://www.ReadioActive.com

Psalm 119:105
Amplified Bible, Classic Edition (AMPC)

*Your word is a lamp to my feet
and a
light to my path.*

INTRODUCTION

This daily reading plan and journal is a tool to help you read the Bible cover to cover THIS YEAR!

Your journey starts today, as we work through the entire Bible, cover to cover, book by book, Genesis to Revelation. The beginning of every month has a quick reference list of the verses you will read. Check the boxes to mark off each day as you progress through the assigned scripture. Use the areas provided below the date and your assigned reading as your blank canvas to reflect, create, and journal.

We pray that through your reading and journaling, you enhance your understanding of the Bible, and create a deeper relationship with God.

Journaling is great at helping you process what you are reading, boosting memory and comprehension and strengthening self-discipline. This reading plan and journal is designed to inspire you to create from the word of God, and express your feelings, thoughts, ideas, or notes by doodling, drawing, coloring, and writing your way through the Bible.

If this daily Bible reading plan & journal has inspired you, please share it with others.

Table of Contents

Introduction 4

January 7

February 19

March 30

April 42

May 53

June 65

July 77

August 89

September 101

October 113

November 125

December 137

January 2019

January 1st
☐ Genesis 1-3

January 2nd
☐ Genesis 4-7

January 3rd
☐ Genesis 8-11

January 4th
☐ Genesis 12-15

January 5th
☐ Genesis 16-18

January 6th
☐ Genesis 19-21

January 7th
☐ Genesis 22-24

January 8th
☐ Genesis 25-26

January 9th
☐ Genesis 27-29

January 10th
☐ Genesis 30-31

January 11th
☐ Genesis 32-34

January 12th
☐ Genesis 35-37

January 13th
☐ Genesis 38-40

January 14th
☐ Genesis 41-42

January 15th
☐ Genesis 43-45

January 16th
☐ Genesis 46-47

January 17th
☐ Genesis 48-50

January 18th
☐ Exodus 1-3

January 19th
☐ Exodus 4-6

January 20th
☐ Exodus 7-9

January 21st
☐ Exodus 10-12

January 22nd
☐ Exodus 13-15

January 23rd
☐ Exodus 16-18

January 24th
☐ Exodus 19-21

January 25th
☐ Exodus 22-24

January 26th
☐ Exodus 25-27

January 27th
☐ Exodus 28-29

January 28th
☐ Exodus 30-32

January 29th
☐ Exodus 33-35

January 30th
☐ Exodus 36-38

January 31st
☐ Exodus 39-40

GENESIS 1:1
AMPLIFIED BIBLE, CLASSIC EDITION (AMPC)

IN THE BEGINNING GOD (PREPARED, FORMED, FASHIONED, AND) CREATED THE HEAVENS AND THE EARTH.

January 1st — Genesis 1-3

January 2nd — Genesis 4-7

Genesis 8-11 — *January 3rd*

Genesis 12-15 — *January 4th*

Genesis 16-18 — *January 5th*

January 6th — Genesis 19-21

January 7th — Genesis 22-24

January 8th — Genesis 25-26

Genesis 27-29 — *January 9th*

Genesis 30-31 — *January 10th*

Genesis 32-34 — *January 11th*

January 12th — Genesis 35-37

January 13th — Genesis 38-40

January 14th — Genesis 41-42

Genesis 43-45 — January 15th

Genesis 46-47 — January 16th

Genesis 48-50 — January 17th

January 18th — Exodus 1-3

January 19th — Exodus 4-6

January 20th — Exodus 7-9

Exodus 10-12   January 21st

Exodus 13-15   January 22nd

Exodus 16-18   January 23rd

January 24th — Exodus 19-21

January 25th — Exodus 22-24

January 26th — Exodus 25-27

Exodus 28-29 — January 27th

Exodus 30-32 — January 28th

Exodus 33-35 — January 29th

January 30th — Exodus 36-38

January 31st — Exodus 39-40

Notes

February 2019

February 1st
☐ Leviticus 1-4

February 2nd
☐ Leviticus 5-7

February 3rd
☐ Leviticus 8-10

February 4th
☐ Leviticus 11-13

February 5th
☐ Leviticus 14-15

February 6th
☐ Leviticus 16-18

February 7th
☐ Leviticus 19-21

February 8th
☐ Leviticus 22-23

February 9th
☐ Leviticus 24-25

February 10th
☐ Leviticus 26-27

February 11th
☐ Numbers 1-2

February 12th
☐ Numbers 3-4

February 13th
☐ Numbers 5-6

February 14th
☐ Numbers 7

February 15th
☐ Numbers 8-10

February 16th
☐ Numbers 11-13

February 17th
☐ Numbers 14-15

February 18th
☐ Numbers 16-17

February 19th
☐ Numbers 18-20

February 20th
☐ Numbers 21-22

February 21st
☐ Numbers 23-25

February 22nd
☐ Numbers 26-27

February 23rd
☐ Numbers 28-30

February 24th
☐ Numbers 31-32

February 25th
☐ Numbers 33-34

February 26th
☐ Numbers 35-36

February 27th
☐ Deuteronomy 1-2

February 28th
☐ Deuteronomy 3-4

> YOU SHALL NOT TAKE REVENGE OR BEAR ANY GRUDGE AGAINST THE SONS OF YOUR PEOPLE, BUT YOU SHALL LOVE YOUR NEIGHBOR AS YOURSELF. I AM THE LORD.
>
> LEVITICUS 19:18
> AMPLIFIED BIBLE, CLASSIC EDITION (AMPC)

February 1st — Leviticus 1-4

February 2nd — Leviticus 5-7

Leviticus 8-10 — February 3rd

Leviticus 11-13 — February 4th

Leviticus 14-15 — February 5th

February 6th — *Leviticus 16-18*

February 7th — *Leviticus 19-21*

February 8th — *Leviticus 22-23*

Leviticus 24-25 — February 9th

Leviticus 26-27 — February 10th

Numbers 1-2 — February 11th

February 12th   Numbers 3-4

February 13th   Numbers 5-6

February 14th   Numbers 7

Numbers 8-10 — February 15th

Numbers 11-13 — February 16th

Numbers 14-15 — February 17th

February 18th — Numbers 16-17

February 19th — Numbers 18-20

February 20th — Numbers 21-22

Numbers 23-25 — *February 21st*

Numbers 26-27 — *February 22nd*

Numbers 28-30 — *February 23rd*

February 24th — Numbers 31-32

February 25th — Numbers 33-34

February 26th — Numbers 35-36

Deuteronomy 1-2
February 27th

Deuteronomy 3-4
February 28th

Notes

March 2019

March 1st
☐ Deuteronomy 5-7

March 2nd
☐ Deuteronomy 8-10

March 3rd
☐ Deuteronomy 11-13

March 4th
☐ Deuteronomy 14-16

March 5th
☐ Deuteronomy 17-20

March 6th
☐ Deuteronomy 21-23

March 7th
☐ Deuteronomy 24-27

March 8th
☐ Deuteronomy 28-29

March 9th
☐ Deuteronomy 30-31

March 10th
☐ Deuteronomy 32-34

March 11th
☐ Joshua 1-4

March 12th
☐ Joshua 5-8

March 13th
☐ Joshua 9-11

March 14th
☐ Joshua 12-15

March 15th
☐ Joshua 16-18

March 16th
☐ Joshua 19-21

March 17th
☐ Joshua 22-24

March 18th
☐ Judges 1-2

March 19th
☐ Judges 3-5

March 20th
☐ Judges 6-7

March 21st
☐ Judges 8-9

March 22nd
☐ Judges 10-12

March 23rd
☐ Judges 13-15

March 24th
☐ Judges 16-18

March 25th
☐ Judges 19-21

March 26th
☐ Ruth 1-4

March 27th
☐ 1 Samuel 1-3

March 28th
☐ 1 Samuel 4-8

March 29th
☐ 1 Samuel 9-12

March 30th
☐ 1 Samuel 13-14

March 31st
☐ 1 Samuel 15-17

DEUTERONOMY 6:5 (AMPC)
AND YOU SHALL LOVE THE LORD YOUR GOD WITH ALL YOUR [MIND AND] HEART AND WITH YOUR ENTIRE BEING AND WITH ALL YOUR MIGHT.

Deuteronomy 5-7 — March 1st

Deuteronomy 8-10 — March 2nd

March 3rd — Deuteronomy 11-13

March 4th — Deuteronomy 14-16

March 5th — Deuteronomy 17-20

Deuteronomy 21-23 — March 6th

Deuteronomy 24-27 — March 7th

Deuteronomy 28-29 — March 8th

March 9th Deuteronomy 30-31

March 10th Deuteronomy 32-34

March 11th Joshua 1-4

Joshua 5-8 — March 12th

Joshua 9-11 — March 13th

Joshua 12-15 — March 14th

March 15th — Joshua 16-18

March 16th — Joshua 19-21

March 17th — Joshua 22-24

Judges 1-2 — March 18th

Judges 3-5 — March 19th

Judges 6-7 — March 20th

March 21st　　　　　　　　　　　　Judges 8-9

March 22nd　　　　　　　　　　　Judges 10-12

March 23rd　　　　　　　　　　　Judges 13-15

Judges 16-18 — March 24th

Judges 19-21 — March 25th

Ruth 1-4 — March 26th

March 27th — 1 Samuel 1-3

March 28th — 1 Samuel 4-8

March 29th — 1 Samuel 9-12

1 Samuel 13-14   March 30th

1 Samuel 15-17   March 31st

Notes

April 2019

April 1st
☐ 1 Samuel 18-20

April 2nd
☐ 1 Samuel 21-24

April 3rd
☐ 1 Samuel 25-27

April 4th
☐ 1 Samuel 28-31

April 5th
☐ 2 Samuel 1-3

April 6th
☐ 2 Samuel 4-7

April 7th
☐ 2 Samuel 8-12

April 8th
☐ 2 Samuel 13-15

April 9th
☐ 2 Samuel 16-18

April 10th
☐ 2 Samuel 19-21

April 11th
☐ 2 Samuel 22-24

April 12th
☐ 1 Kings 1-2

April 13th
☐ 1 Kings 3-5

April 14th
☐ 1 Kings 6-7

April 15th
☐ 1 Kings 8-9

April 16th
☐ 1 Kings 10-11

April 17th
☐ 1 Kings 12-14

April 18th
☐ 1 Kings 15-17

April 19th
☐ 1 Kings 18-20

April 20th
☐ 1 Kings 21-22

April 21st
☐ 2 Kings 1-3

April 22nd
☐ 2 Kings 4-5

April 23rd
☐ Kings 6-8

April 24th
☐ 2 Kings 9-11

April 25th
☐ 2 Kings 12-14

April 26th
☐ 2 Kings 15-17

April 27th
☐ 2 Kings 18-19

April 28th
☐ 2 Kings 20-22

April 29th
☐ 2 Kings 23-25

April 30th
☐ 1 Chronicles 1-2

1 Samuel 18-20 — April 1st

1 Samuel 21-24 — April 2nd

1 Samuel 25-27 — April 3rd

April 4th
1 Samuel 28-31

April 5th
2 Samuel 1-3

April 6th
2 Samuel 4-7

2 Samuel 8-12
April 7th

2 Samuel 13-15
April 8th

2 Samuel 16-18
April 9th

April 10th — 2 Samuel 19-21

April 11th — 2 Samuel 22-24

April 12th — 1 Kings 1-2

1 Kings 3-5
April 13th

1 Kings 6-7
April 14th

1 Kings 8-9
April 15th

April 16th — 1 Kings 10-11

April 17th — 1 Kings 12-14

April 18th — 1 Kings 15-17

1 Kings 18-20   April 19th

1 Kings 21-22   April 20th

2 Kings 1-3   April 21st

April 22nd — 2 Kings 4-5

April 23rd — 2 Kings 6-8

April 24th — 2 Kings 9-11

2 Kings 12-14 — April 25th

2 Kings 15-17 — April 26th

2 Kings 18-19 — April 27th

April 28th — 2 Kings 20-22

April 29th — 2 Kings 23-25

April 30th — 1 Chronicles 1-2

May 2019

May 1st
☐ 1 Chronicles 3-5

May 2nd
☐ 1 Chronicles 6

May 3rd
☐ 1 Chronicles 7-8

May 4th
☐ 1 Chronicles 9-11

May 5th
☐ 1 Chronicles 12-14

May 6th
☐ 1 Chronicles 15-17

May 7th
☐ 1 Chronicles 18-21

May 8th
☐ 1 Chronicles 22-24

May 9th
☐ 1 Chronicles 25-27

May 10th
☐ 1 Chronicles 28 - 2 Chronicles 1

May 11th
☐ 2 Chronicles 2-5

May 12th
☐ 2 Chronicles 6-8

May 13th
☐ 2 Chronicles 9-12

May 14th
☐ 2 Chronicles 13-17

May 15th
☐ 2 Chronicles 18-20

May 16th
☐ 2 Chronicles 21-24

May 17th
☐ 2 Chronicles 25-27

May 18th
☐ 2 Chronicles 28-31

May 19th
☐ 2 Chronicles 32-34

May 20th
☐ 2 Chronicles 35-36

May 21st
☐ Ezra 1-3

May 22nd
☐ Ezra 4-7

May 23rd
☐ Ezra 8-10

May 24th
☐ Nehemiah 1-3

May 25th
☐ Nehemiah 4-6

May 26th
☐ Nehemiah 7

May 27th
☐ Nehemiah 8-9

May 28th
☐ Nehemiah 10-11

May 29th
☐ Nehemiah 12-13

May 30th
☐ Esther 1-5

May 31st
☐ Esther 6-10

2 CHRONICLES 7:14
AMPLIFIED BIBLE, CLASSIC EDITION (AMPC)

IF MY PEOPLE, WHO ARE CALLED BY MY NAME, SHALL HUMBLE THEMSELVES, PRAY, SEEK, CRAVE, AND REQUIRE OF NECESSITY MY FACE AND TURN FROM THEIR WICKED WAYS, THEN WILL I HEAR FROM HEAVEN, FORGIVE THEIR SIN, AND HEAL THEIR LAND.

May 1st — 1 Chronicles 3-5

May 2nd — 1 Chronicles 6

1 Chronicles 7-8
May 3rd

1 Chronicles 9-11
May 4th

1 Chronicles 12-14
May 5th

May 6th   1 Chronicles 15-17

May 7th   1 Chronicles 18-21

May 8th   1 Chronicles 22-24

1 Chronicles 25-27
May 9th

1 Chronicles 28-2 Chronicles 1
May 10th

2 Chronicles 2-5
May 11th

May 12th — 2 Chronicles 6-8

May 13th — 2 Chronicles 9-12

May 14th — 2 Chronicles 13-17

2 Chronicles 18-20 — May 15th

2 Chronicles 21-24 — May 16th

2 Chronicles 25-27 — May 17th

May 18th — 2 Chronicles 28-31

May 19th — 2 Chronicles 32-34

May 20th — 2 Chronicles 35-36

Ezra 1-3 — May 21st

Ezra 4-7 — May 22nd

Ezra 8-10 — May 23rd

May 24th   Nehemiah 1-3

May 25th   Nehemiah 4-6

May 26th   Nehemiah 7

Nehemiah 8-9 — May 27th

Nehemiah 10-11 — May 28th

Nehemiah 12-13 — May 29th

May 30th — Esther 1-5

May 31st — Esther 6-10

Notes

June 2019

June 1st
☐ Job 1-4

June 2nd
☐ Job 5-7

June 3rd
☐ Job 8-10

June 4th
☐ Job 11-13

June 5th
☐ Job 14-16

June 6th
☐ Job 17-20

June 7th
☐ Job 21-23

June 8th
☐ Job 24-28

June 9th
☐ Job 29-31

June 10th
☐ Job 32-34

June 11th
☐ Job 35-37

June 12th
☐ Job 38-39

June 13th
☐ Job 40-42

June 14th
☐ Psalm 1-8

June 15th
☐ Psalm 9-16

June 16th
☐ Psalm 17-20

June 17th
☐ Psalm 21-25

June 18th
☐ Psalm 26-31

June 19th
☐ Psalm 32-35

June 20th
☐ Psalm 36-39

June 21st
☐ Psalm 40-45

June 22nd
☐ Psalm 46-50

June 23rd
☐ Psalm 51-57

June 24th
☐ Psalm 58-65

June 25th
☐ Psalm 66-69

June 26th
☐ Psalm 70-73

June 27th
☐ Psalm 74-77

June 28th
☐ Psalm 78-79

June 29th
☐ Psalm 80-85

June 30th
☐ Psalm 86-89

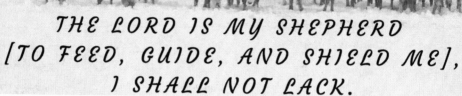

PSALM 23:1
AMPLIFIED BIBLE, CLASSIC EDITION (AMPC)

THE LORD IS MY SHEPHERD
[TO FEED, GUIDE, AND SHIELD ME],
I SHALL NOT LACK.

June 1st — Job 1-4

June 2nd — Job 5-7

Job 8-10 — June 3rd

Job 11-13 — June 4th

Job 14-16 — June 5th

June 6th — Job 17-20

June 7th — Job 21-23

June 8th — Job 24-28

Job 29-31 — June 9th

Job 32-34 — June 10th

Job 35-37 — June 11th

June 12th — *Job 38-39*

June 13th — *Job 40-42*

June 14th — *Psalm 1-8*

Psalm 9-16 — June 15th

Psalm 17-20 — June 16th

Psalm 21-25 — June 17th

June 18th — Psalm 26-31

June 19th — Psalm 32-35

June 20th — Psalm 36-39

Psalm 40-45 *June 21st*

Psalm 46-50 *June 22nd*

Psalm 51-57 *June 23rd*

June 24th — Psalm 58-65

June 25th — Psalm 66-69

June 26th — Psalm 70-73

Psalm 74-77 — June 27th

Psalm 78-79 — June 28th

Psalm 80-85 — June 29th

June 30th — Psalm 86-89

Notes

Halfway Point

YOU'RE DOING GREAT!

July 2019

July 1st
☐ Psalm 90-95

July 2nd
☐ Psalm 96-102

July 3rd
☐ Psalm 103-105

July 4th
☐ Psalm 106-107

July 5th
☐ Psalm 108-114

July 6th
☐ Psalm 115-118

July 7th
☐ Psalm 119:1-88

July 8th
☐ Psalm 119:89-176

July 9th
☐ Psalm 120-132

July 10th
☐ Psalm 133-139

July 11th
☐ Psalm 140-145

July 12th
☐ Psalm 146-150

July 13th
☐ Proverbs 1-3

July 14th
☐ Proverbs 4-6

July 15th
☐ Proverbs 7-9

July 16th
☐ Proverbs 10-12

July 17th
☐ Proverbs 13-15

July 18th
☐ Proverbs 16-18

July 19th
☐ Proverbs 19-21

July 20th
☐ Proverbs 22-23

July 21st
☐ Proverbs 24-26

July 22nd
☐ Proverbs 27-29

July 23rd
☐ Proverbs 30-31

July 24th
☐ Ecclesiastes 1-4

July 25th
☐ Ecclesiastes 5-8

July 26th
☐ Ecclesiastes 9-12

July 27th
☐ Song of Solomon 1-8

July 28th
☐ Isaiah 1-4

July 29th
☐ Isaiah 5-8

July 30th
☐ Isaiah 9-12

July 31st
☐ Isaiah 13-17

**PROVERBS 3:5
AMPLIFIED BIBLE, CLASSIC EDITION
(AMPC)**
LEAN ON, TRUST IN, AND BE CONFIDENT IN THE LORD WITH ALL YOUR HEART AND MIND AND DO NOT RELY ON YOUR OWN INSIGHT OR UNDERSTANDING.

July 1st — *Psalm 90-95*

July 2nd — *Psalm 96-102*

Psalm 103-105 — July 3rd

Psalm 106-107 — July 4th

Psalm 108-114 — July 5th

July 6th — Psalm 115-118

July 7th — Psalm 119:1-88

July 8th — Psalm 119:89-176

Psalm 120-132 — July 9th

Psalm 133-139 — July 10th

Psalm 140-145 — July 11th

July 12th — Psalm 146-150

July 13th — Proverbs 1-3

July 14th — Proverbs 4-6

Proverbs 7-9
July 15th

Proverbs 10-12
July 16th

Proverbs 13-15
July 17th

July 18th   Proverbs 16-18

July 19th   Proverbs 19-21

July 20th   Proverbs 22-23

Proverbs 24-26 — July 21st

Proverbs 27-29 — July 22nd

Proverbs 30-31 — July 23rd

July 24th — Ecclesiastes 1-4

July 25th — Ecclesiastes 5-8

July 26th — Ecclesiastes 9-12

Song of Solomon 1-8 — July 27th

Isaiah 1-4 — July 28th

Isaiah 5-8 — July 29th

July 30th Isaiah 9-12

July 31st Isaiah 13-17

Notes

August 2019

August 1st
☐ Isaiah 18-22

August 2nd
☐ Isaiah 23-27

August 3rd
☐ Isaiah 28-30

August 4th
☐ Isaiah 31-35

August 5th
☐ Isaiah 36-41

August 6th
☐ Isaiah 42-44

August 7th
☐ Isaiah 45-48

August 8th
☐ Isaiah 49-53

August 9th
☐ Isaiah 54-58

August 10th
☐ Isaiah 59-63

August 11th
☐ Isaiah 64-66

August 12th
☐ Jeremiah 1-3

August 13th
☐ Jeremiah 4-6

August 14th
☐ Jeremiah 7-9

August 15th
☐ Jeremiah 10-13

August 16th
☐ Jeremiah 14-17

August 17th
☐ Jeremiah 18-22

August 18th
☐ Jeremiah 23-25

August 19th
☐ Jeremiah 26-29

August 20th
☐ Jeremiah 30-31

August 21st
☐ Jeremiah 32-34

August 22nd
☐ Jeremiah 35-37

August 23rd
☐ Jeremiah 38-41

August 24th
☐ Jeremiah 42-45

August 25th
☐ Jeremiah 46-48

August 26th
☐ Jeremiah 49-50

August 27th
☐ Jeremiah 51-52

August 28th
☐ Lamentations 1:1-3:36

August 29th
☐ Lamentations 3:37-5:22

August 30th
☐ Ezekiel 1-4

August 31st
☐ Ezekiel 5-8

ISAIAH 40:31 (AMPC)
BUT THOSE WHO WAIT FOR THE LORD [WHO EXPECT, LOOK FOR, AND HOPE IN HIM] SHALL CHANGE AND RENEW THEIR STRENGTH AND POWER; THEY SHALL LIFT THEIR WINGS AND MOUNT UP [CLOSE TO GOD] AS EAGLES [MOUNT UP TO THE SUN]; THEY SHALL RUN AND NOT BE WEARY, THEY SHALL WALK AND NOT FAINT OR BECOME TIRED.

August 1st — Isaiah 18-22

August 2nd — Isaiah 23-27

Isaiah 28-30　　　　　　August 3rd

Isaiah 31-35　　　　　　August 4th

Isaiah 36-41　　　　　　August 5th

August 6th — Isaiah 42-44

August 7th — Isaiah 45-48

August 8th — Isaiah 49-53

Isaiah 54-58 — August 9th

Isaiah 59-63 — August 10th

Isaiah 64-66 — August 11th

August 12th — Jeremiah 1-3

August 13th — Jeremiah 4-6

August 14th — Jeremiah 7-9

Jeremiah 10-13 — August 15th

Jeremiah 14-17 — August 16th

Jeremiah 18-22 — August 17th

August 18th — Jeremiah 23-25

August 19th — Jeremiah 26-29

August 20th — Jeremiah 30-31

Jeremiah 32-34 — August 21st

Jeremiah 35-37 — August 22nd

Jeremiah 38-41 — August 23rd

August 24th — Jeremiah 42-45

August 25th — Jeremiah 46-48

August 26th — Jeremiah 49-50

Jeremiah 51-52 — August 27th

Lamentations 1:1-3:36 — August 28th

Lamentations 3:37-5:22 — August 29th

August 30th — Ezekiel 1-4

August 31st — Ezekiel 5-8

Notes

September 2019

September 1st
☐ Ezekiel 9-12

September 2nd
☐ Ezekiel 13-15

September 3rd
☐ Ezekiel 16-17

September 4th
☐ Ezekiel 18-20

September 5th
☐ Ezekiel 21-22

September 6th
☐ Ezekiel 23-24

September 7th
☐ Ezekiel 25-27

September 8th
☐ Ezekiel 28-30

September 9th
☐ Ezekiel 31-33

September 10th
☐ Ezekiel 34-36

September 11th
☐ Ezekiel 37-39

September 12th
☐ Ezekiel 40-42

September 13th
☐ Ezekiel 43-45

September 14th
☐ Ezekiel 46-48

September 15th
☐ Daniel 1-3

September 16th
☐ Daniel 4-6

September 17th
☐ Daniel 7-9

September 18th
☐ Daniel 10-12

September 19th
☐ Hosea 1-7

September 20th
☐ Hosea 8-14

September 21st
☐ Joel 1-3

September 22nd
☐ Amos 1-5

September 23rd
☐ Amos 6-9

September 24th
☐ Obadiah-Jonah 4

September 25th
☐ Micah 1-7

September 26th
☐ Nahum 1-3

September 27th
☐ Habakkuk-Zephaniah 3

September 28th
☐ Haggai 1-2

September 29th
☐ Zechariah 1-7

September 30th
☐ Zechariah 8-14

JONAH 1:17 (AMPC)

NOW THE LORD HAD PREPARED AND APPOINTED A GREAT FISH TO SWALLOW UP JONAH.

AND JONAH WAS IN THE BELLY OF THE FISH THREE DAYS AND THREE NIGHTS.

September 1st — Ezekiel 9-12

September 2nd — Ezekiel 13-15

Ezekiel 16-17 — September 3rd

Ezekiel 18-20 — September 4th

Ezekiel 21-22 — September 5th

September 6th Ezekiel 23-24

September 7th Ezekiel 25-27

September 8th Ezekiel 28-30

Ezekiel 31-33
September 9th

Ezekiel 34-36
September 10th

Ezekiel 37-39
September 11th

September 12th — Ezekiel 40-42

September 13th — Ezekiel 43-45

September 14th — Ezekiel 46-48

Daniel 1-3   September 15th

Daniel 4-6   September 16th

Daniel 7-9   September 17th

September 18th — Daniel 10-12

September 19th — Hosea 1-7

September 20th — Hosea 8-14

Joel 1-3
September 21st

Amos 1-5
September 22nd

Amos 6-9
September 23rd

September 24th — *Obadiah-Jonah 4*

September 25th — *Micah 1-7*

September 26th — *Nahum 1-3*

Habakkuk-Zephaniah 3 — September 27th

Haggai 1-2 — September 28th

Zechariah 1-7 — September 29th

September 30th — Zechariah 8-14

Notes

October 2019

October 1st
☐ Malachi 1-4

October 2nd
☐ Matthew 1-4

October 3rd
☐ Matthew 5-6

October 4th
☐ Matthew 7-8

October 5th
☐ Matthew 9-10

October 6th
☐ Matthew 11-12

October 7th
☐ Matthew 13-14

October 8th
☐ Matthew 15-17

October 9th
☐ Matthew 18-19

October 10th
☐ Matthew 20-21

October 11th
☐ Matthew 22-23

October 12th
☐ Matthew 24-25

October 13th
☐ Matthew 26

October 14th
☐ Matthew 27-28

October 15th
☐ Mark 1-3

October 16th
☐ Mark 4-5

October 17th
☐ Mark 6-7

October 18th
☐ Mark 8-9

October 19th
☐ Mark 10-11

October 20th
☐ Mark 12-13

October 21st
☐ Mark 14

October 22nd
☐ Mark 15-16

October 23rd
☐ Luke 1

October 24th
☐ Luke 2-3

October 25th
☐ Luke 4-5

October 26th
☐ Luke 6-7

October 27th
☐ Luke 8-9

October 28th
☐ Luke 10-11

October 29th
☐ Luke 12-13

October 30th
☐ Luke 14-16

October 31st
☐ Luke 17-18

MATTHEW 28:19 (AMPC)

GO THEREFORE AND MAKE DISCIPLES OF ALL NATIONS, BAPTIZING THEM IN[B] THE NAME OF THE FATHER AND OF THE SON AND OF THE HOLY SPIRIT,

October 1st — Malachi 1-4

October 2nd — Matthew 1-4

Matthew 5-6 — October 3rd

Matthew 7-8 — October 4th

Matthew 9-10 — October 5th

October 6th Matthew 11-12

October 7th Matthew 13-14

October 8th Matthew 15-17

Matthew 18-19 — October 9th

Matthew 20-21 — October 10th

Matthew 22-23 — October 11th

October 12th — Matthew 24-25

October 13th — Matthew 26

October 14th — Matthew 27-28

Mark 1-3   *October 15th*

Mark 4-5   *October 16th*

Mark 6-7   *October 17th*

October 18th — Mark 8-9

October 19th — Mark 10-11

October 20th — Mark 12-13

Mark 14 — October 21st

Mark 15-16 — October 22nd

Luke 1 — October 23rd

October 24th — Luke 2-3

October 25th — Luke 4-5

October 26th — Luke 6-7

Luke 8-9 — October 27th

Luke 10-11 — October 28th

Luke 12-13 — October 29th

October 30th — Luke 14-16

October 31st — Luke 17-18

Notes

November 2019

November 1st
☐ Luke 19-20

November 2nd
☐ Luke 21-22

November 3rd
☐ Luke 23-24

November 4th
☐ John 1-2

November 5th
☐ John 3-4

November 6th
☐ John 5-6

November 7th
☐ John 7-8

November 8th
☐ John 9-10

November 9th
☐ John 11-12

November 10th
☐ John 13-15

November 11th
☐ John 16-18

November 12th
☐ John 19-21

November 13th
☐ Acts 1-3

November 14th
☐ Acts 4-6

November 15th
☐ Acts 7-8

November 16th
☐ Acts 9-10

November 17th
☐ Acts 11-13

November 18th
☐ Acts 14-15

November 19th
☐ Acts 16-17

November 20th
☐ Acts 18-20

November 21st
☐ Acts 21-23

November 22nd
☐ Acts 24-26

November 23rd
☐ Acts 27-28

November 24th
☐ Romans 1-3

November 25th
☐ Romans 4-7

November 26th
☐ Romans 8-10

November 27th
☐ Romans 11-13

November 28th
☐ Romans 14-16

November 29th
☐ 1 Corinthians 1-4

November 30th
☐ 1 Corinthians 5-8

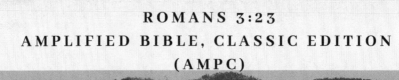

ROMANS 3:23
AMPLIFIED BIBLE, CLASSIC EDITION
(AMPC)

SINCE ALL HAVE SINNED AND ARE FALLING SHORT OF THE HONOR AND GLORY WHICH GOD BESTOWS AND RECEIVES.

November 1st — Luke 19-20

November 2nd — Luke 21-22

Luke 23-24 — November 3rd

John 1-2 — November 4th

John 3-4 — November 5th

November 6th — John 5-6

November 7th — John 7-8

November 8th — John 9-10

John 11-12

November 9th

John 13-15

November 10th

John 16-18

November 11th

November 12th — John 19-21

November 13th — Acts 1-3

November 14th — Acts 4-6

Acts 7-8
November 15th

Acts 9-10
November 16th

Acts 11-13
November 17th

November 18th — Acts 14-15

November 19th — Acts 16-17

November 20th — Acts 18-20

Acts 21-23 — November 21st

Acts 24-26 — November 22nd

Acts 27-28 — November 23rd

November 24th — Romans 1-3

November 25th — Romans 4-7

November 26th — Romans 8-10

Romans 11-13
November 27th

Romans 14-16
November 28th

1 Corinthians 1-4
November 29th

November 30th

1 Corinthians 5-8

Notes

December 2019

December 1st
☐ 1 Corinthians 9-11

December 2nd
☐ 1 Corinthians 12-14

December 3rd
☐ 1 Corinthians 15-16

December 4th
☐ 2 Corinthians 1-4

December 5th
☐ 2 Corinthians 5-9

December 6th
☐ 2 Corinthians 10-13

December 7th
☐ Galatians 1-3

December 8th
☐ Galatians 4-6

December 9th
☐ Ephesians 1-3

December 10th
☐ Ephesians 4-6

December 11th
☐ Philippians 1-4

December 12th
☐ Colossians 1-4

December 13th
☐ 1 Thessalonians 1-5

December 14th
☐ 2 Thessalonians 1-3

December 15th
☐ 1 Timothy 1-6

December 16th
☐ 2 Timothy 1-4

December 17th
☐ Titus-Philemon

December 18th
☐ Hebrews 1-6

December 19th
☐ Hebrews 7-10

December 20th
☐ Hebrews 11-13

December 21st
☐ James 1-5

December 22nd
☐ 1 Peter 1-5

December 23rd
☐ 2 Peter 1-3

December 24th
☐ 1 John 1-5

December 25th
☐ 2 John-Jude

December 26th
☐ Revelation 1-3

December 27th
☐ Revelation 4-8

December 28th
☐ Revelation 9-12

December 29th
☐ Revelation 13-16

December 30th
☐ Revelation 17-19

December 31st
☐ Revelation 20-22

EPHESIANS 2:8
AMPLIFIED BIBLE, CLASSIC EDITION
(AMPC)

FOR IT IS BY FREE GRACE (GOD'S UNMERITED FAVOR) THAT YOU ARE SAVED (DELIVERED FROM JUDGMENT AND MADE PARTAKERS OF CHRIST'S SALVATION) THROUGH [YOUR] FAITH. AND THIS [SALVATION] IS NOT OF YOURSELVES [OF YOUR OWN DOING, IT CAME NOT THROUGH YOUR OWN STRIVING], BUT IT IS THE GIFT OF GOD;

December 1st   *1 Corinthians 9-11*

December 2nd   *1 Corinthians 12-14*

1 Corinthians 15-16
December 3rd

2 Corinthians 1-4
December 4th

2 Corinthians 5-9
December 5th

December 6th — 2 Corinthians 10-13

December 7th — Galatians 1-3

December 8th — Galatians 4-6

Ephesians 1-3
December 9th

Ephesians 4-6
December 10th

Philippians 1-4
December 11th

December 12th — Colossians 1-4

December 13th — 1 Thessalonians 1-5

December 14th — 2 Thessalonians 1-3

1 Timothy 1-6   December 15th

2 Timothy 1-4   December 16th

Titus-Philemon   December 17th

December 18th — Hebrews 1-6

December 19th — Hebrews 7-10

December 20th — Hebrews 11-13

James 1-5
December 21st

1 Peter 1-5
December 22nd

2 Peter 1-3
December 23rd

December 24th   *1 John 1-5*

December 25th   *2 John-Jude*

December 26th   *Revelation 1-3*

Revelation 4-8 — December 27th

Revelation 9-12 — December 28th

Revelation 13-16 — December 29th

December 30th Revelation 17-19

December 31st Revelation 20-22

Notes

You Made It To The End

Let's Do It Again

Next Year

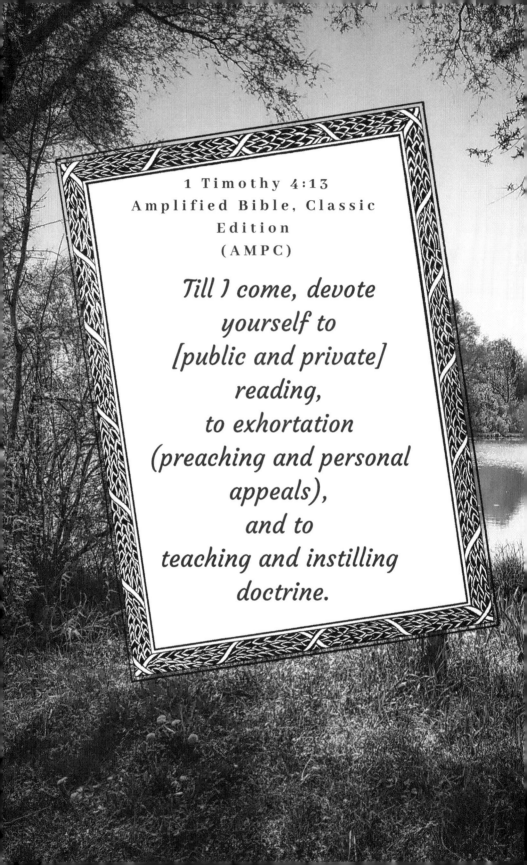

Made in the USA
Columbia, SC
21 August 2023